Henry's House

Your Body
Boogers and All

Philip Ardagh
illustrated by Mike Gordon

PSS!
PRICE STERN SLOAN
An Imprint of Penguin Group (USA) Inc.

For Freddie, of course!
P.A.

GROSSET & DUNLAP
Published by the Penguin Group
Penguin Group (USA) Inc., 375 Hudson Street, New York, New York 10014, USA
Penguin Group (Canada), 90 Eglinton Avenue East, Suite 700, Toronto, Ontario M4P 2Y3, Canada
(a division of Pearson Penguin Canada Inc.)
Penguin Books Ltd., 80 Strand, London WC2R 0RL, England
Penguin Group Ireland, 25 St. Stephen's Green, Dublin 2, Ireland
(a division of Penguin Books Ltd.)
Penguin Group (Australia), 250 Camberwell Road, Camberwell, Victoria 3124, Australia
(a division of Pearson Australia Group Pty. Ltd.)
Penguin Books India Pvt. Ltd., 11 Community Centre, Panchsheel Park, New Delhi—110 017, India
Penguin Group (NZ), 67 Apollo Drive, Rosedale, North Shore 0632, New Zealand
(a division of Pearson New Zealand Ltd.)
Penguin Books (South Africa) (Pty.) Ltd., 24 Sturdee Avenue,
Rosebank, Johannesburg 2196, South Africa

Penguin Books Ltd., Registered Offices:
80 Strand, London WC2R 0RL, England

Text copyright © 2009 Philip Ardagh. Illustrations copyright © 2009 Mike Gordon.
First printed in Great Britain in 2009 by Scholastic UK. First published in the United States in 2010 by
Price Stern Sloan, a division of Penguin Young Readers Group, 345 Hudson Street, New York, New York 10014.
PSS! is a trademark of Penguin Group (USA) Inc. Manufactured in Singapore.

Library of Congress Cataloging-in-Publication Data is available.

ISBN 978-0-8431-2230-5   10 9 8 7 6 5 4 3 2 1

Philip Ardagh and Mike Gordon are regular visitors to Henry's House. Philip (the one with the beard) keeps a note of everything that's going on, and even reads a mind or two. Mike (the one without the beard) sketches whatever he sees, however fantastical it may be . . . and together they bring you the adventures of Henry, an ordinary boy in an extraordinary house!

Contents

Welcome to Henry's House!

The human skeleton

The smallest bone in the human body is the stirrup. We have one in each ear.

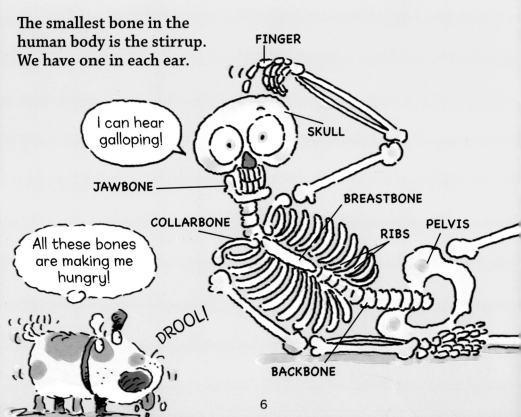

The longest bone in the human body is the thighbone.

THIGHBONE
KNEECAP
SHINBONE
TOES
ANKLEBONE

Dr. Ray's bony facts

Babies are born with around 350 bones. When they are fully grown, they only have 206.

Don't look at me!

As we grow older, some smaller bones join together to make bigger ones.

My skeleton is on the outside of my body!

Bones are hard on the outside...

...and spongy on the inside.

The spongy stuff is called marrow.

(Bones are three-quarters water!)

A BUG

Along with animals such as gorillas, we humans have opposable thumbs.

This means that we can touch the tips of our thumbs to the tips of all our fingers on the same hand.

This makes us good at using tools and playing the piano.

I can't play the piano. I'm not very musical.

?????!

Muscles are what get us moving, lifting, running, jumping, and even sitting.

Our most powerful muscles are on the sides of our mouth. They're just right for biting!

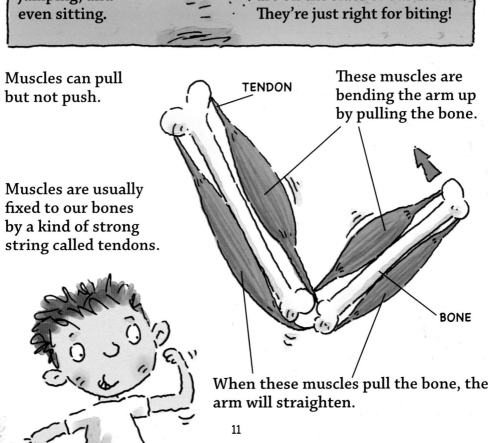

Muscles can pull but not push.

TENDON

These muscles are bending the arm up by pulling the bone.

Muscles are usually fixed to our bones by a kind of strong string called tendons.

BONE

When these muscles pull the bone, the arm will straighten.

11

Skin underfoot

Your skin keeps your insides IN and the outside OUT.

It covers your body with a waterproof oil.

Your skin pumps out salty water, called sweat, to cool you down.

Touch sensors in your skin help you tell rough things from smooth ones.

ARGH!!! A giant flea!

ARGH!!! A tiny dog!

Welcome to the world of human skin! It's made up of two layers.

EPIDERMIS   DERMIS

Pain sensors make you feel pain when your skin is hurt.

OUCH!

Pressure sensors help you feel how hard your skin is pushing or being pushed!

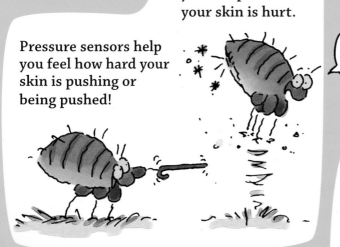

And you can guess what heat sensors do!

Heaven nose!

By the way...

Drool! Slurp!

Some scientists don't think that umami (a savory kind of taste)
is really its own separate taste type.

18

Have a look at your face in the bottom of this saucepan, Henry, and stick out your tongue.

If you insist!

Our tongues are covered in sensors called tastebuds.

Your spit helps you to taste your food as well as making it easier to swallow.

Parts of the tongue pick up some flavors more easily than others.

Sweet things taste sweetest when put on the tip of the tongue.

The way food smells and feels affects the way it tastes.

A breath of fresh air

I shouldn't have eaten all those sausages!

Phew! I ate so much, I can hardly breathe!

Did you know that we breathe in air because we need the oxygen in it?

GROAN!

BURP!

PUFF!

PANT!

LUNGS this way

HENRY'S HOUSE

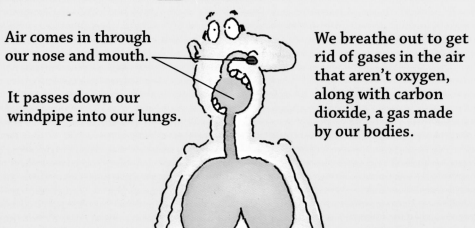

Air comes in through our nose and mouth.

It passes down our windpipe into our lungs.

We breathe out to get rid of gases in the air that aren't oxygen, along with carbon dioxide, a gas made by our bodies.

If we didn't breathe out, we'd blow up like balloons!

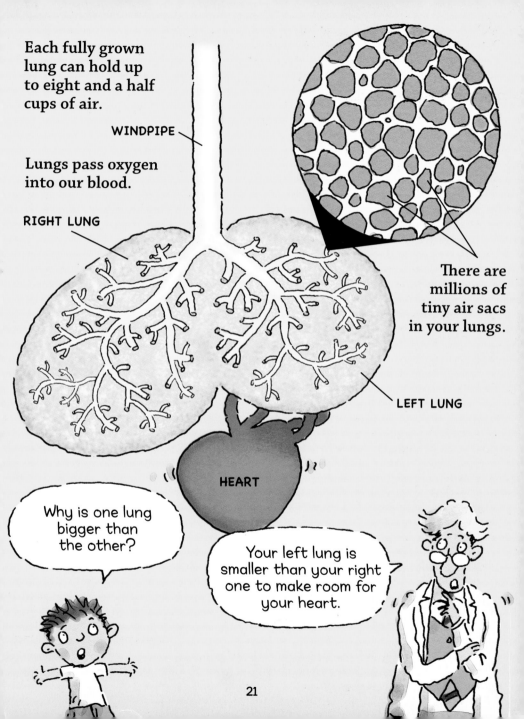

The heart is a large muscle. It pumps blood around the body.

The average heart beats about 100,000 times a day. That's over 36 million times a year!

Without a heart to pump it, our blood would not flow.

Women's hearts beat faster than men's.

An adult human heart can build up enough pressure to squirt blood up to 40 feet. SQUI RTSQQU IRTSS SSSSSSSSS SSSSS SQQURTTTS QQQQQQ QQQQQQQ QQRTTT TFP TZSTUIGI BIFXBWFZ ZBXWWW ghdvsjhdhdf djhdfgjkshf jfhfkjfh kf jfkfsksrurf jhfs….>>>>>>::&%^\$%\$£%^

SPLUTTER!

KERCHUNK!

PHUT! PHUT!

FIZZ!

PHUT!

BANG!

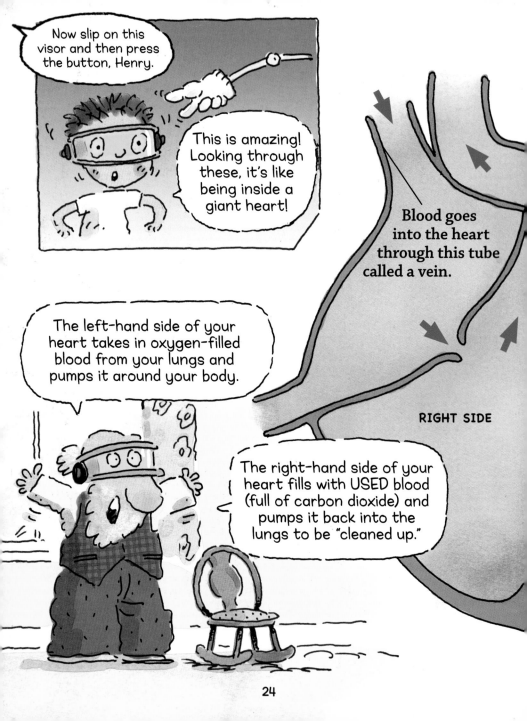

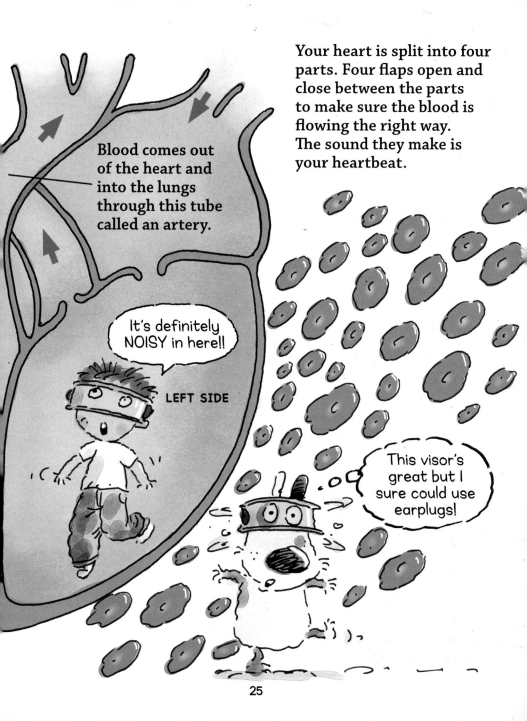

Your heart is split into four parts. Four flaps open and close between the parts to make sure the blood is flowing the right way. The sound they make is your heartbeat.

Blood comes out of the heart and into the lungs through this tube called an artery.

It's definitely NOISY in here!!

LEFT SIDE

This visor's great but I sure could use earplugs!

The blood! The blood!

Magnus Boffin's visors are incredible!

Some of his inventions work much better than others! He is very smart, though.

Could he tell us why some bruises turn black-and-blue—like this old one on my arm?

We need to scoot down to the cellar and drop in on the Bates family—the house's resident blood experts.

HI, GUYS. HOW'S IT HANGING?

Our resident blood experts are VAMPIRE BATS?

Human blood contains red blood cells, white blood cells, and platelets.

RED BLOOD CELL

PLATELETS

WHITE BLOOD CELL

There are around 250 million red blood cells in a drop of blood, along with 13 million platelets and 375,000 white blood cells.

Red blood cells carry oxygen around the body.

They look a bit like doughnuts. Would you like one?

Er—blerch! No, thanks. I'm not hungry!

White blood cells are like soldiers in an army, defending our bodies against tiny invaders called germs.

ATTACK!!!

WHITE BLOOD CELL

Excuse me! You're not getting through without the password!

27

What have we ear?

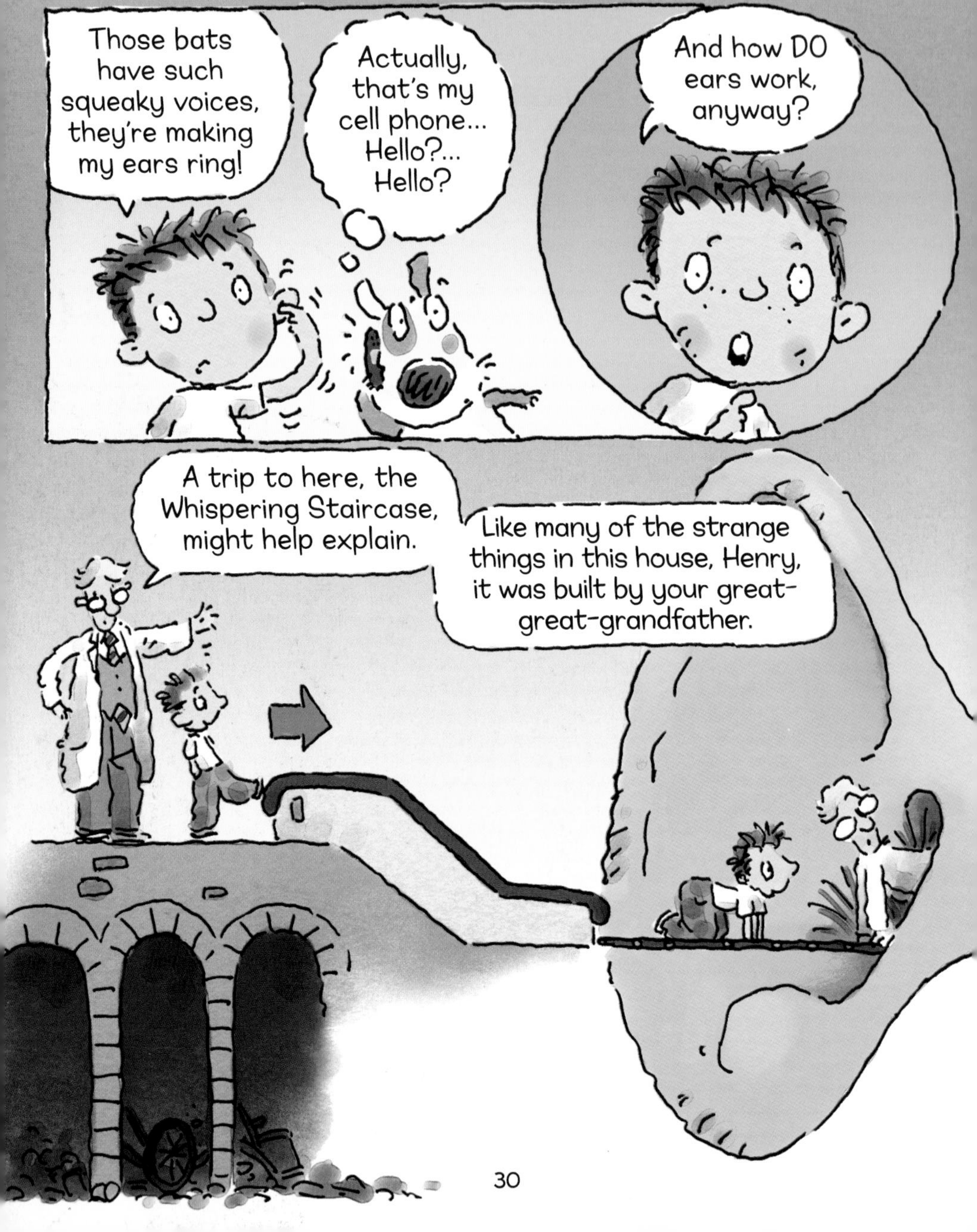

32

HELP! It's not as easy as it looks.

YERCH! Someone carved those statues of famous composers out of earwax!

Earwax helps protect your ears, but TOO MUCH earwax can stop you from hearing properly.

BALANCING ACT

Inside your ears, there are tiny tubes filled with liquid.

As you move around, the liquid moves around, too, bending special tiny hairs.

The hairs send messages to your brain. They tell it which way you move, to help you keep your balance.

This part of the ear sends sound signals to the brain.

Nerves help send the signals to the brain.

Something to shout about!

WAIL!!!

What's that noise?

Oh no! That's Madame Fortissimo, the used-to-be famous singer.

BURP!

Excuse me!

The windpipe carries air to your lungs.

LUNGS

The voice box is the part of the throat used for speaking.

To speak, shout, laugh, or sing, air from your lungs is blown past two thick bands in your voice box.

The air makes the bands vibrate, creating a sound. The bands are short and tight when you make a high sound.

The bands are longer and looser when you make a low sound.

By changing the shape of your mouth...

...and moving your tongue and lips...

...you can change the sounds once they've left your voice box.

If I play dead, will she stop making those scary faces?

BURP!

Oops!

People burp about fifteen times a day. It's just unwanted gas escaping through our mouths!

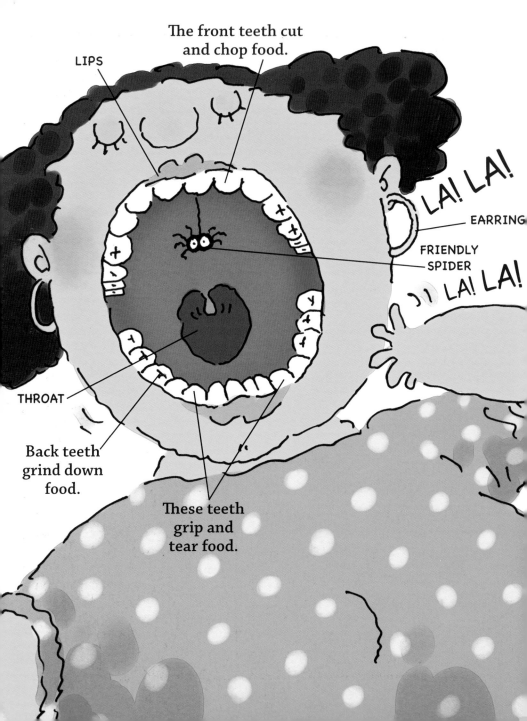

Hard to swallow

Oh, it's you two again...

THREE. Can't you count?

Cookie, I was wondering what happens to our food once our teeth have chomped it.

More foodie questions. Great! When you eat, your tongue rolls your food into small, mushy balls.

These balls are forced into the tube that leads to your stomach and you swallow them down.

Bands of muscles squeeze the food along. You could even eat standing on your head.

Which must be useful if you're a bat...

Stop looking at me like that, Mothball!!!

Once you've swallowed, food takes up to three days to travel through lots of tubes...

...A grown-up's digestive system is about 30 FEET long!!!

This lovely "MR. FOOD" chart will help me to explain.

MR. FOOD'S INCREDIBLE JOURNEY

1. First, Mr. Food travels from your mouth to your stomach.

STOMACH

2. In your stomach, Mr. Food is squeezed and mixed with special juices ... turning him into a thick mush. The liver makes juices to help digest Mr. Food.

3. Next, Mr. Food passes into a tube called your small intestine. Here, useful chemicals are taken out of him and sent around your body.

KIDNEYS

4. The large intestine soaks up water and sends it to your kidneys.

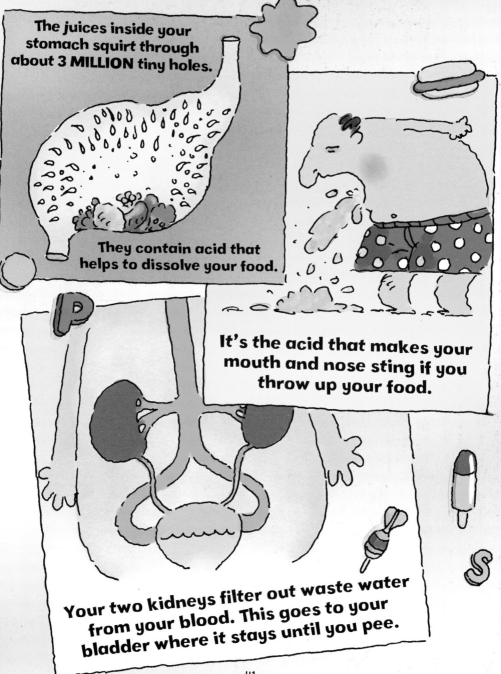

The juices inside your stomach squirt through about 3 **MILLION** tiny holes.

They contain acid that helps to dissolve your food.

It's the acid that makes your mouth and nose sting if you throw up your food.

Your two kidneys filter out waste water from your blood. This goes to your bladder where it stays until you pee.

Eyeball to eyeball

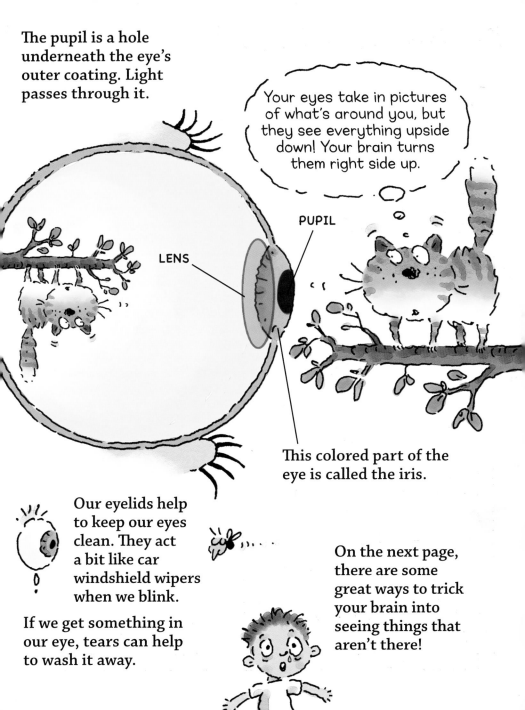

The pupil is a hole underneath the eye's outer coating. Light passes through it.

Your eyes take in pictures of what's around you, but they see everything upside down! Your brain turns them right side up.

PUPIL

LENS

This colored part of the eye is called the iris.

Our eyelids help to keep our eyes clean. They act a bit like car windshield wipers when we blink.

If we get something in our eye, tears can help to wash it away.

On the next page, there are some great ways to trick your brain into seeing things that aren't there!

Don't believe your eyes!

When you look at this ring, it's obviously all one shade of gray.

When you split the ring, it may look a little lighter on the left than on the right.

When you slide it down, the two halves look like totally different shades of gray.

Your brain keeps putting gray dots in the white circles, even though they're not there!

The first illusion is called Koffka's Ring. It's an example of our brain trying to make sense of what it sees and getting all confused!

This is weird, Jaggers!

???

Brain box!

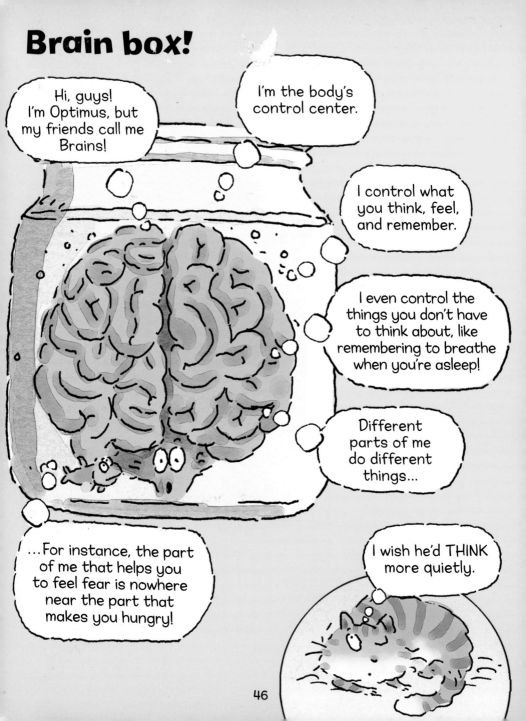

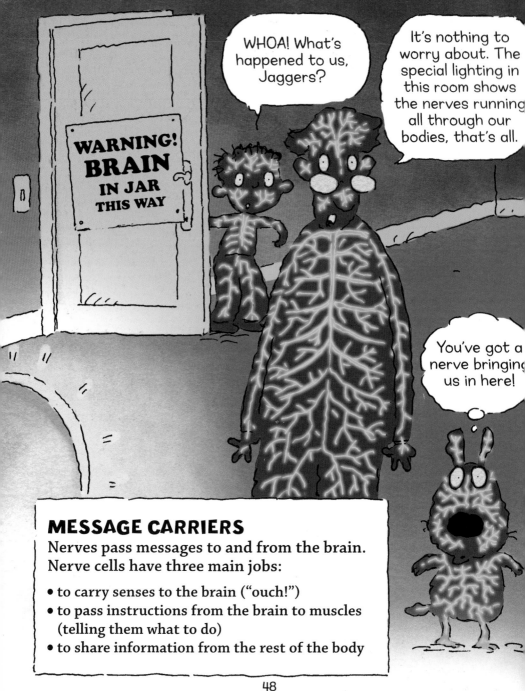

MESSAGE CARRIERS

Nerves pass messages to and from the brain.
Nerve cells have three main jobs:

- to carry senses to the brain ("ouch!")
- to pass instructions from the brain to muscles (telling them what to do)
- to share information from the rest of the body

MY SUPERSMART BRAIN
by Henry

There are BILLIONS of nerve cells in my brain.

They can receive around 100,000 messages a second.

These messages can be turned into my memories.

Messages can zip around at up to 270 miles an hour!

You can see a ball, catch it, and throw it back in a few seconds, even though the messages making this happen have to pass through MILLIONS of nerve cells.

And, at the same time, I can think about all those slobbery DOGGY GERMS on the ball!

DRIBBLE!

DROOL!

The body fights back

How does our body fight germs, Jaggers?

Let's ask some in person! There are different types, you know... After you...

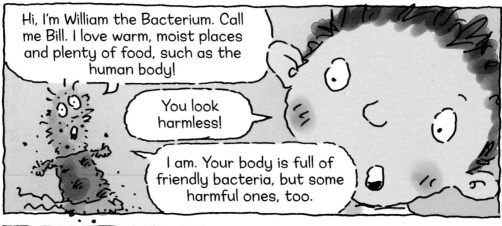

Hi, I'm William the Bacterium. Call me Bill. I love warm, moist places and plenty of food, such as the human body!

You look harmless!

I am. Your body is full of friendly bacteria, but some harmful ones, too.

I'm Veronica the Virus. I invade your cells and force them into making more viruses!

That sounds like a pretty mean trick, Veronica!

Not really, I'm just doing my job!

51

Grow up!

Hi, Henry! I'm Wally Walnut from Room 404. My battle isn't with germs but with growing older... and I reckon I'm WINNING!

I feel GREAT!

Eardrums losing their bounce, making it harder to hear.

Hair falling out. The hair that's left is turning white.

Teeth getting worn down.

Eyesight getting worse.

Skin wrinkling, because it has stretched over the years.

95 today

If you think I'm OLD, you should meet my DAD!

Bones getting thinner and weaker.

Blood vessels weakening.

Wally is in great shape for his age but, as we get older, our cells stop working so hard and fix themselves more slowly.

Joints getting stiff.

52

Fit 'n' healthy

55

Sweet dreams

Thanks for everything, Jaggers! It's been a COOL day! I think I'll turn in early.

No one knows for sure why we dream. Perhaps our brains are trying to make sense of the day.

We have dreams every night (even if we don't always remember them). Most of us have about 1,000 dreams a year!

The human body

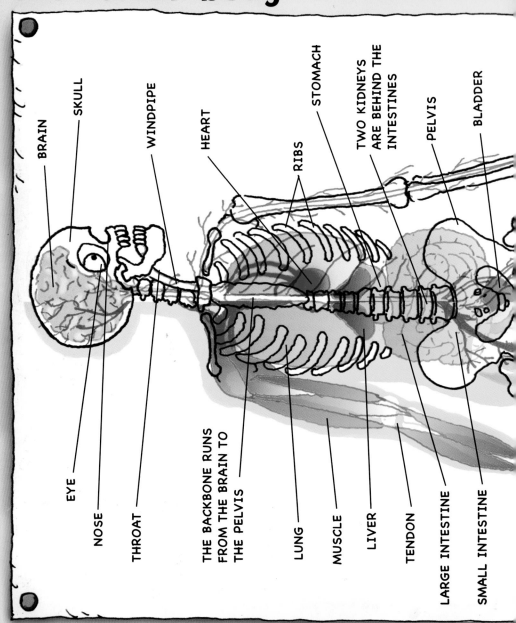

BRAIN

SKULL

WINDPIPE

HEART

STOMACH

RIBS

TWO KIDNEYS
ARE BEHIND THE
INTESTINES

PELVIS

BLADDER

EYE

NOSE

THROAT

THE BACKBONE RUNS
FROM THE BRAIN TO
THE PELVIS

LUNG

MUSCLE

LIVER

TENDON

LARGE INTESTINE

SMALL INTESTINE

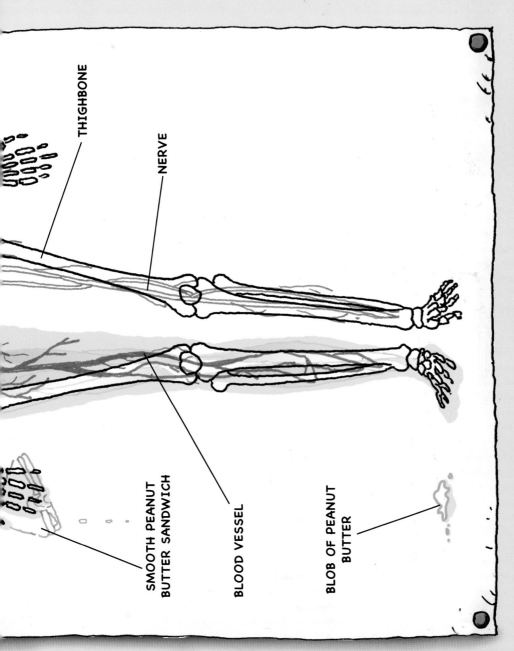

THIGHBONE

NERVE

SMOOTH PEANUT
BUTTER SANDWICH

BLOOD VESSEL

BLOB OF PEANUT
BUTTER

Glossary

Acid: a very strong liquid that breaks down the food inside your stomach.

Allergy: a response to certain substances, such as pollen, food, or medication. It could make you sneeze, make your eyes itch, or even make you break out in a rash.

Blood vessel: the narrow tube in your body through which blood flows.

Ear canal: the tube connecting the outer and middle parts of your ear.

Earwax: the yellowish, sticky stuff, which guards the ear canal.

Enamel: the hard, white surface of your teeth.

Filter: a way to separate the things you want from things you don't.

Gland: a group of cells that make important juices that your body needs to work properly.

Nerve: a thin strand that passes instructions and information to and from your brain, telling you how to move and feel.

Nostril: the hole at the bottom of your nose, which allows air and smells in and out.

Sensor: a part of your body that tells your brain when you touch or feel something, including heat.

Snot: the sticky and slippery stuff in your nose and windpipe, which catches dust and bacteria, stopping them from getting into your body.

3-D (three-dimensional): something that has three dimensions (height, width, and depth) instead of being flat like a drawing.

Index

Henry's House

We hope you enjoyed your visit

to Henry's House!

Come back soon!

Look out for: Dinosaurs
Fangs and All